S0-AXU-951

TO:

FROM:

Photograph courtesy CBS/Getty Images

Copyright © 2002
Peter Pauper Press, Inc.
202 Mamaroneck Avenue
White Plains, NY 10601

Published by arrangement with
The Doubleday Broadway Publishing Group,
a division of Random House, Inc.
Originally published by Doubleday
under the title FATHERHOOD by Bill Cosby.

ISBN 0-88088-181-X
Printed in China
7  6  5  4  3

Visit us at www.peterpauper.com

# Bill Cosby *on*
# FATHERHOOD

**The new father, of course,** feels that his mere impregnation of his mate, done every day by otters and apes, is Olympic gold medal stuff.

**Even if he's afraid of garter snakes, he feels positively heroic.** He feels that he and his wife have nobly created something that will last.

He never thinks that they may have created one of the top ten underachievers in their town.

**If you really love your wife, her pregnancy is a time to test your attention span.** You have to pay attention when she says, "It's moving! Wake up and feel it!" You have to respond as if she's pointing out a replay of a touchdown pass.

**A**lthough you don't have to agree to carry [the baby] for her, you *should* make an effort to keep helping her and to keep expressing your love. Make sure that she sits in comfortable chairs; and then help her out of the chair when it's time to leave, or else you'll find yourself in the street without her because she'll still be in the chair, flapping her arms and trying to get airborne.

**Like every man, of course, I had no understanding of how a labor pain really feels. . . .** When the second big pain hit, she cried out and stood up in the stirrups. . . . And at the next contraction, she told everyone in the delivery room that my parents were never married.

Then she continued breathing while I continued cheering from the sidelines:

**"PUSH! PUSH! PUSH!"**

**B**ecause you are feeding both the child and the floor, raising this child will be expensive. The Lord was wise enough to make a woman's pregnancy last nine months. If it were shorter, people with temporary insanity might have two or three kids a year, and they would be wiped out before the first one had learned to talk.

A father today has disposable diapers and plastic bottles. The only thing left to invent is a plastic toy that will hit the floor and then bounce back into the crib.

Before we had children, my wife and I felt educated. She was a college graduate, a child psychology major with a B-plus average, which means, if you ask her a question about a child's behavior, she will give you eighty-five percent of the answer. And I was a physical education major with a child psychology minor at Temple, which means if you ask me a question about a child's behavior, I will advise you to tell the child to take a lap.

**[W]hat will set your child apart from the others is its name.** Always end the name of your child with a vowel, so that when you yell, the name will carry.

I do not see how a mother can hang out of her window and do anything much with a cry of "Torvald!" . . . My own father violated this rule by giving me a name that ended in "t," but you have to admit that this name was an exception. He called me Jesus Christ. Often he turned to me and said, "Jesus Christ!"

My brother had a name that also ended in a consonant: "Lookdammit." Addressing the two of us, my father would say, "Lookdammit, stop jumping on the furniture! Jesus Christ, can't you ever be still?"

In spite of these names for my brother and me, my father did try hard not to curse, an effort that often rendered him semi-articulate. Having to squelch the profanities that he dearly wanted to lavish on me reduced him to saying such things as, "If you ever . . . because you're a . . . and I'll be . . . because it's just too . . . and I swear I'll . . ."

For many years, in fact, I thought my father was a man unable to complete a sentence. **I made him swallow curses like after-dinner mints.**

I always corrected
my father respectfully
because, although he
never gave me a
beating, he did often
hit for distance.
Many times when
I was flying by, a
neighbor would say,

**"Tell your father
I said hello."**

"I brought you into this world," my father would say, "and I can take you out. It don't make no difference to me. I'll just make another one like you."

In spite of my father's feelings, I presume that you still have decided to have a child instead of a hamster. A hamster, however, would give you more privacy in the bathroom. . . . A new father quickly learns that his child invariably comes to the bathroom at precisely the times when he's in there, as if he needed company. The only way for this father to be certain of bathroom privacy is to shave at the gas station.

# People who have no children say they love them because children are so truthful.

Well, I have done extensive fieldwork with five children and can tell you as scientific fact that the only time they tell the truth is when they are in pain.

A baby, however, sells itself and needs no advertising copy; few people can resist it. There is something about babyness that brings out the softness in people and makes them want to hug and protect this small thing . . .

I guess the real reason that my wife and I had children is the same reason that Napoleon had for invading Russia: it seemed like a good idea at the time.

# You know why John D. Rockefeller had all that money?

Because he had only one child, so he didn't have to spend ninety thousand dollars on Snoopy pens and Superhero mugs and Smurf pajamas and Barbie Ferraris.

My wife and I . . . did not have children so they could yell at each other all over the house, moving me to say,

# What's the problem?

"She's waving her foot in my room," my daughter replied.

"And something like that *bothers* you?"

"Yes, I don't *want* her foot in my room."

"Well," I said, dipping into my storehouse of paternal wisdom, "why don't you just close the door?"

"Then I can't see what she's doing!"

It doesn't make any difference how much money a father earns, his name is always Dad-Can-I; and he always wonders whether these little people were born to beg. I bought each of my five children everything up to a Rainbow Brite jacuzzi and still I kept hearing "Dad, can I get . . . Dad, can I go . . . Dad, can I buy . . ."

Sometimes, at three or four in the morning, I open the door to one of the children's bedrooms and watch the light softly fall across their little faces. And then I quietly kneel beside one of the beds and just look at the girl lying there because she is so beautiful. And because she is not begging. Kneeling there, I listen reverently to the sounds of her breathing.

And then
she wakes up
and says,
"Dad,
can I . . ."

"Okay," I said to all five one day, "go get into the car." All five then ran to the same car door, grabbed the same handle, and spent the next few minutes beating each other up. Not one of them had the intelligence to say, "Hey, *look*. There are three more doors." The dog, however, was already inside.

**W**henever your kids are out of control, you can take comfort from the thought that even God's omnipotence did not extend to His kids. After creating the heaven, the earth, the oceans, and the entire animal kingdom, God created Adam and Eve. And the first thing He said to them was "Don't." . . .

"Don't what?" Adam replied

"Don't eat the forbidden fruit."

"Forbidden fruit? Really? Where is it?"

Is this beginning to sound familiar? You never realized that the pattern of your life had been laid down in the Garden of Eden. . . .

A few minutes later, God saw the kids having an apple break and He was angry.

"Didn't I *tell* you not to eat that fruit?" the First Parent said.

"Uh-huh," Adam replied.

"Then why *did* you?"

"I don't know," Adam said.

At least he didn't say, "No problem."

"All right then, get out of

here! Go forth, become fruitful, and multiply!"

This was not a blessing but a curse: God's punishment was that Adam and Eve should have children of their own.

**A**t the peak of Michael Jackson's fame, when I had girls of six and ten who lived amid Jackson paraphernalia, I discovered that I could use *him* as a proxy disciplinarian.

**"Michael Jackson loves all his fans,** but he has a special feeling for the ones who eat broccoli," I said one night at

dinner, and two of his fans
quickly swallowed both that
story and broccoli too.

I learned what many young men have learned: if you leave your clothes on the floor of your room long enough, you can wait your mother out. Sooner or later, she will pick them up and wash them for you.

[Y]ou are *not* the boss of this house that you want the children out of within thirty years and you are not allowed to give them permission for anything. When one of them comes to you and says, "Dad, can I go explore the Upper Nile?" your answer must be,

"Go ask your mother." . . .

However, I have seen the boss's job and I don't want it, for sometimes the boss ends up sitting alone in a room and talking to herself as if the enemy were there: "What do you *mean* you don't want to do it? When I tell you to do something, you *do* it and you don't stand there practicing for law school!"

**B**efore we were married, my wife was a stunningly beautiful woman. Today she is a stunningly beautiful woman . . . who has conversations with herself. She also sounds like my mother: "I'm gonna knock you into the middle of next week!" The middle of next week, by the way, is where their father wouldn't mind going: I would have four days by myself.

# [W]henever a child starts to say, "Dad, can I . . ."

even though it's my name, I always reply, "What did your mother say?"

And even if the child says that she got permission, I still say, "Very fine. Just bring me a note from your mother. It doesn't have to be notarized. A simple signature and date will do."

You see, the wives *pretend* to turn over the child-raising job to us fathers, but they don't really mean it. One day, my wife said to me,

## "He's *your* child. I wash my hands of him."

Where is this sink where you can wash your hands of a child? I want to wash my hands too, and then the boy can go free.

[In] the boy's room, we had that nice thoughtful talk I mentioned earlier, the one in which he could not remember when he had shaved his head; and then, being a father who likes to probe to the very souls of those I love, I said,

"So tell me, son, how are things?"

"Okay," he said.

"Is there any problem you'd like to discuss with Dad?"

"It's okay."

And, as every father knows,

## "Okay" means *"I haven't killed anyone."*

**N**o matter how calmly you try to referee, parenting will eventually produce bizarre behavior, and I'm not talking about the kids.

*Their* behavior is always normal, a norm of acting incomprehensibly with sweetly blank looks. But *you* will find yourself strolling down the road to the funny farm—like my mother, who used to get so angry that she would forget my name:

"All right, come *over* here, Bar-uh, Bernie . . . uh, uh—Biff . . . uh—what *is* your name, boy?

And don't lie to me, 'cause you
live here and I'll find out who
you are and take a stick and
knock your brains out!"

If the new American father feels bewildered and even defeated, let him take comfort from the fact that whatever he does in any fathering situation has a fifty percent chance of being right. Having five children has taught me a truth as cosmic as any that you can find on a mountain in Tibet:

**There are no absolutes in raising children.**

In any stressful situation, fathering is always a roll of the dice. The game may be messy, but I have never found one with more rewards and joys.

You know the only people who are always sure about the proper way to raise children?

**Those who've never had any.**

Okay, so I *haven't* been Solomon, perhaps because I've felt more like Noah, just lost at sea. But the truth is that parents are not really interested in justice. They just want quiet.

No matter how much the pressure on your spinal cord builds up, never let these small people know that you have gone insane. There is an excellent reason for this: they want the house; and at the first sign that something is wrong with you, they will take you right to a home.

At the moment that a boy of thirteen is turning toward girls, a girl of thirteen is turning on her mother. This girl can get rather unreasonable, often saying such comical things as,

## "Listen, this is my *life!*"

This remark is probably her response to her mother having said, "You are *not* going to South Carolina alone to see a boy that you talked to on the telephone for ninety seconds."

"But Mother, I've *got* to see him. This is my *life* and you're *ruining* it! *You're* from the olden days. *Your* life is *over!*"

When your fifteen-year-old son does speak, he often says one of two things: either "Okay," which, as we know, means "I haven't killed anyone," or "No problem."

[My son's] failing his native tongue piqued my curiosity, so I said, "How can you fail English?"

"Yeah," he replied.

Hoping to get an answer that had something to do with the question, I said again, "Please tell me: how can you fail English?"

"I don't know," he said.

"Son, you didn't really fail *English*, did you? You failed handing in reports on time, right? Because you can understand people who speak English, can't you? And when you talk, *they* can understand you, can't they? So the teacher *understood* what you had

written but just didn't care for
the way you put it, right? You
just failed *organization*, right?
I mean, the teacher who failed
you in English also said, 'He
can do the work,' right? It's
just that you don't *want* to do it
yet. And all it'll take is maybe
leaving you out in the wilder-
ness with no food or money in

the middle of winter. Just a dime to make a collect call saying that you're ready to study."

"No problem," he said.

**A**nd here's the whole challenge of being a parent. Even though your kids will consistently do the exact opposite of what you tell them to do, you have to keep loving them just as much.

Let me repeat: nothing is harder for a parent than getting your kids to do the right thing. There is such a rich variety of ways for you to fail: by using threats, by using bribery, by using reason, by using example, by using blackmail, or by pleading for mercy. Walk into any bus terminal in America and you will see men on benches poignantly staring into space with the looks of generals who have just surrendered. They are fathers who have run out of ways to get their children to do the right thing.

"My boy is having his problems being a serious student," I told Eddie.

"Well, your studying is very important," Eddie said, while the boy sat smiling a smile that said: an old person is about to hand out some Wisdom. Could this please be over fast? "You know, a jet plane burns its greatest energy taking off; but once it reaches its cruising altitude, it burns less fuel. Just like studying. If you're constantly taking off and landing, you're going to burn more fuel as opposed to taking off and staying up there and maintaining that altitude."

A few days later, I ran into my son in the house. . . .

"How's school?" I said.
Without a word, he raised his arm and laid his palm down and flat like a plane that had leveled off. He suddenly knew it was the only way to fly.

*There are many good moments in fathering, but few better than that.*

**The father of a daughter, especially one in her teens, will find that she doesn't like to be seen walking with him on the street.** In fact, she will often ask him to walk a few paces behind. The father should not take this outdoor demotion personally; it is simply a matter of clothes. His are rotten. Every American daughter is an authority on fashion, and one of the things she knows is that her father dresses like somebody in the Mummers Parade.

In schools,
you can always
identify the
children who
were dressed by
their fathers.

**S**uch children should have signs pinned on the strange attire that say:

*Please do not scorn or mock me. I was dressed by my father, who sees colors the way Beethoven heard notes.*

Remember Cosby's First Law of Intergenerational Perversity?

Well, it also applies to being hip. Anything that *you* like cannot possibly be something your kids like too, so it cannot possibly be hip.

I recently met a man and woman who had been married for fifty years and they told me a story with enough horror for Brian DePalma. Their forty-six-year-old son had just moved back in with them, bringing his two kids, one who was twenty-three and one who was twenty-two. All three of them were out of work.

"And that," I told my wife, "is why there is death."

Who wants to be seven hundred years old and look out the window and see your six-hundred-year-old son coming home to live with you? Bringing his two four-hundred-year-old kids.

Every time you attend a graduation, you hear a dean or president say, "And so, young men and women, as you go forth . . ."

For years, I had thought that forth meant going out into the world on their own; I had thought that forth meant leaving home.

## But then I discovered that I was wrong.

**Every time that they go forth, they come back, so forth must mean home.**

My father, however, gave to forth its old traditional meaning. On the day I was graduated from college, he presented to me a Benrus watch and then he said with a smile, "All right, now give me the keys to the house."

"Why, Dad?" I replied. "Because you're going forth, which is any direction but to this house."

Immortality?
Now that I have
had five children,
my only hope is
that they all are
out of the house
before I die.

**W**e have shown all five of them constant attention, faith, and love. Like all parents since Adam and Eve (who never quite seemed to understand sibling rivalry), we have made mistakes; but we've learned from them, we've learned from the *kids,* and we've all grown together. [We] will always stumble and bumble from time to time, but we do have the kind of mutual trust that I wish the United Nations had. And, with breaks for a little hollering, we smile a lot.